SP… STORIES FOR CURIOUS KIDS

YOUNG READERS STEM EDITION

Printed in the USA.

Book illustrations and cover design by Davor Ratkovic

Contents

The Night the Lights Went Out in New York City

It can be scary when the power goes out in our houses. Sometimes, in a big storm, our houses will lose electricity. It can be dark without the lights. It might be hot or cold if the heater or air conditioner doesn't work. Having electricity for our houses sure makes us grateful!

On a night in November 1965, many people were going home from work in New York City. Over 800,000 people were riding on subways below the ground. That's pretty crowded. All of a sudden, DARKNESS!!! Even the bright lights of Times Square went out. It was pitch black everywhere. Below the ground, people were stuck in the dark subway tunnels. Way up in giant skyscrapers, people were trapped inside elevators. What a mess! What happened to cause this?

A power grid helps send electricity to where it is needed.

EARLY READER EDITION

One of the buttons on a power grid got set too low. This meant that it got overloaded and turned off. After that, it became like a game of dominoes. Have you ever lined up a bunch of dominoes in a pattern? You hit the first one, and as it falls, it knocks over the next one. Before you know it, all the dominoes are falling! The electricity was the same way. A power grid would shut down, which would cause the next power grid to shut down. Before too long... DARKNESS.

Within ten minutes, over thirty million people in eight states would be affected by the electricity turning off. The people riding on subways would find flashlights and help each other find a way to get back up to the streets. Nurses held flashlights so doctors could finish their surgeries. People worked together and helped each other on this crazy night of darkness.

It took all night, almost thirteen hours, but finally, everyone got the electricity back to their homes and businesses. It turned out to be one of the lowest nights of crime ever for New York City. People were too busy being helpful and kind in the darkness to do bad things. Even in the darkness, people let their inner lights shine.

2 Two Very Silly Scientists

Do you know what a rivalry is? It's when people are competing to be the best at something. Many people think about sports team rivalries. That is when two sports teams each want to be the best at their sport. History is full of rivalries too. This rivalry had to do with bones!

In the late 1800s, people were finding dinosaur bones. They were learning about new species as they discovered more bones. Scientists were very excited. They wanted to learn more.

Two scientists each wanted to be the best. Edward Cope and Othniel Marsh both loved to dig up dinosaur bones. They liked to talk about science and fossils. When they first met, they were friends. They shared information and wrote letters to each other. That didn't last for long!

Edward invited Othniel to come to a dig site with him. Othniel was sneaky. He paid workers to help him find more dinosaur bones. This made Edward mad. Edward told the newspapers that Othniel wasn't a good scientist. He also went to Kansas to dig for bones. He chose to dig in the same exact spot that Othniel was digging. The two were in competition again!

One time, Edward was constructing a completely new dinosaur. He put the head on the tail instead of the neck. It was an honest mistake. Othniel reported it to the newspapers. He wanted them to think Edward wasn't smart.

During this time, a lot of dinosaur bones were being found

out west. Othniel and Edward both wanted to be part of this. They packed up their crews and headed west. This is when the bone wars really got going.

Each man wanted to be the one to find the most fossils. They each wanted to be the best. They used sneaky ways to try to do this. They spied on each

other. They stole each other's workers. They bribed people to keep secrets about new fossils. They even destroyed fossils to prevent each other from finding them. They were always saying mean things about each other in the newspapers. These two very smart men spent a lot of time being mean to each other!

Later in life, when they both died, Edward had discovered fifty-six new species. Othniel had discovered eighty. Before he died, Edward sent one last request to Othniel. He wanted to compare their brain sizes after they were dead! During this time in history, scientists thought that the bigger your brain was, the smarter you were. Edward wanted to prove that he was smarter than Othniel. Othniel refused to compare their brain sizes.

The bone wars were an interesting time for scientists. A lot of new discoveries were made. Scientists learned a lot about dinosaurs. Some people think the bone wars helped the public become more interested in fossils. The silly fighting between the two scientists did get a lot of attention. But just think how much better it might have been if these two smart men had worked together. They might have discovered even more if they had been helping each other.

3

Record Breaking Brother and Sister

What if I told you that a nineteen-year-old girl was the youngest person to ever travel all the way around the earth? She flew an airplane all by herself around the whole world! Then, only two months later, her younger brother did the same thing. He also flew an airplane around the whole world. He was only sixteen years old when he started. He is the youngest person to ever complete this journey.

Wow! These two siblings must be really brave. They must really like to fly airplanes. They do. Zara and Mack Rutherford grew up around airplanes. Their mom and dad were both pilots. Zara remembers helping her dad fly airplanes even when she was a little girl. The family spent a lot of time flying airplanes together.

Why did these two want to fly around the world? They both like adventure. They want to inspire other kids to do things they love to do. Only five percent of airline pilots are girls. Zara wants to change that. She wants other girls to see that they can fly airplanes, too. She wants to inspire other girls to love science and math the way she does.

Mack was the youngest person to become a professional pilot. When he was only fifteen years old, he got his pilot's license. He likes to meet other kids who want to change the world. He wants to show that young people can make a difference.

Both Zara and Mack's journeys took them to many amazing spots in the world.

They traveled in the airplane alone, but met many new friends on their journey. They got to see some beautiful places. Zara said seeing the world was amazing and beautiful.

The airplanes each sibling flew were small planes designed for flying long distances. They are called Sharks. They are lightweight, and they are very

fast. They can fly 186 miles per hour!

Zara's trip took one hundred fifty-five days. She got to visit forty-one countries on five continents. Mack's journey was also five months long. Mack visited fifty-two countries on five continents. Both of their journeys had some delays due to weather and other unplanned events. One night, Mack even had to land on a deserted

island! He had to camp out all alone with only seagulls for company.

Zara and Mack both learned a lot during their trips. They learned about hard work and not giving up. Their stories inspire kids to do great things. Even though they are young, kids can have big dreams. If they work hard and stay focused, kids can achieve amazing things. Kids can help change the world in big and small ways.

4

The Love of a Sister

Do you have any brothers or sisters? Sometimes, brothers and sisters fight, but mostly, they love each other. They want the best for their family. This is the story of two sisters who loved each other and wanted to make their dreams come true.

Marie and Bronislawa Sklodowska lived with their

family in Poland. Their family was full of lots of love. Their parents did not have a lot of money, but they knew that school was important. They encouraged the girls to study hard.

As the girls got older, the family had a problem. Both of these smart girls wanted to attend the university. But where they lived in Poland, girls weren't allowed at the universities! If they wanted to attend school, they would have to go far away, and it would be very expensive.

Their parents couldn't afford to send Marie and Bronislawa

to a university. They felt so sad about it. Marie and Bronislawa came up with a plan. They wanted to look out for each other. They wanted to make both of their dreams come true.

Bronislawa was the oldest girl. The plan was that she would go to Paris to study at a university. Marie would stay home and work. She would pay for Bronislawa to go to school. When Bronislawa finished school, she would get a job. Then she would pay for Marie to go to school.

The plan worked! It took lots of time and patience. Marie worked as a tutor and as a nanny. She studied at night so she would keep learning. Bronislawa worked hard. She became a doctor. Finally, it was Marie's turn to go to university.

She worked very hard in school. Sometimes, she was so focused on her studies that she forgot to eat! She wanted to live close to school so she could study all the time. Her apartment could be very cold. Sometimes Marie had to wear all of her clothes to stay warm.

Marie was very smart and loved science. She wanted to study chemistry. She met another scientist named Pierre Curie. They fell in love and got married. They worked together and made a lot of important discoveries.

Marie Curie became one of the most important scientists

in history. She and her husband discovered radium and polonium. Marie was the first woman to be awarded a Nobel Prize. This is a huge honor given to people who make a big impact on the world. Several years later, she was awarded a second Nobel Prize.

Marie was smart and hardworking. She discovered many new things and helped many people learn more about science. Her work changed the world. It all started because two sisters loved each other and wanted to help each other make their dreams come true.

5

Why Fly When You Can Swim?

One of the most famous ocean scientists learned his love of the ocean by accident. When Jacques Cousteau was a little boy, he wanted to be a pilot. He wanted to soar above the clouds and look down at the earth below.

When he was old enough, he went into flight training. He loved it! But then he was in a terrible car accident. He was very hurt. It looked like he would never be able to be a military pilot.

Jacques started swimming to help himself get stronger after the accident. He made a pair of goggles to make swimming in the ocean easier. He discovered a whole new world under the water. Jacques was excited again! Even if he couldn't be a pilot, he found something he loved doing even more.

He began to explore the ocean anywhere he could. He loved

learning about all the creatures and plants. He liked sharing the beauty of the ocean. He got an underwater camera. Jacques began to make movies about the ocean. Most people had never seen the ocean or what lived in it. They loved learning about all the ocean creatures.

Jacques filmed all over the shores of France. He wanted to see more. He wanted to be able to film more places. He got a giant boat and hired a crew. His family went with him, and they traveled in the boat all over the world. Jacques was the first person to really study whales and dolphins. He learned that whales and dolphins could "talk" to each other using echolocation. Jacques invented scuba gear so he could spend a long time underwater. He was always learning and building new things.

He loved being able to share the ocean with people who couldn't see it. Jacques made movies and TV shows with all the great things he found. Imagine if you had never seen a picture of a dolphin, octopus,

or giant turtle. It would be so cool to see these things for the first time. Thanks to Jacques Cousteau, many people got to see ocean creatures for the very first time.

The ocean meant everything to Jacques. It made him sad to see pollution hurting the ocean and its creatures. He got people to think about how their actions might be hurting the ocean. He asked them to make good choices. This is called

conservation. Jacques was one of the first people to inspire others to take better care of the ocean.

Jacques's story shows us that it's okay if things don't go as planned. There might be something better out there for us. Jacques thought he wanted to be a pilot, but he changed the world with his love of the ocean. It's important to find something you really enjoy doing. It's really cool if you can share it with others.

The First Water Gun

Do you like to play with toy water guns in the summer? Maybe you like to spray your friends. Or maybe you like to get sprayed! The Super Soaker is one of the best water guns for getting wet. It can be a lot of fun to blast water. Who came up with the idea for the Super Soaker water gun?

Lonnie Johnson was a super smart kid. He liked to build robots and tinker with new inventions. Once he tried to make rocket fuel in his kitchen. He almost burned down the house! I'll bet his mom wasn't too happy.

When he was in high school, he entered a contest. He built a robot he named Linex. Linex was on wheels. It could move and spin all around. It even had arms and wrists that could twist and move. Lonnie's robot won first place in the science contest. This was a big deal. When Lonnie was in school, Black and White people went to separate schools. Lonnie was the only Black kid to enter the contest. He didn't let this stop him. He knew he was smart and that his robot could win.

When Lonnie grew up, he worked for NASA. He worked in their lab that built spaceships. One day he was tinkering at home in his basement. He was working on building a part for NASA. He accidentally shot a stream of water across the room. Lonnie thought this might make a really fun toy. The idea for the Super Soaker was born!

Lonnie started to build his new project when he would get home from work. He worked in the basement for several months. When he finished his first water gun, he handed it to his seven-year-old daughter. She got to blast everyone in the neighborhood with this fun toy!

Lonnie needed help if he was going to get his water gun into toy stores. He reached out to a toy company. At the meeting, the toy people asked if the water gun worked. Lonnie shot a stream of water across the room. Everyone got excited. This looked like fun!

The toy company helped Lonnie sell his water gun. Everyone wanted one! Thirty years later, people still buy Super Soaker water guns. It has earned over one billion dollars. It's even in the National Toy Hall of Fame. Lonnie's story reminds us to stay curious and do things that make us excited. Don't let your differences get you down. You are smart and you can do incredible things.

What's Really Down There?

Marie Tharp was a girl who loved rocks. She loved looking at maps. Do you know what she loved most of all? Oceans! Marie thought the oceans were so interesting. It wasn't the fish or ocean creatures that interested her the most. Marie was interested in the bottom of the ocean.

Back then, everybody thought the bottom of the ocean was just flat and filled with mud. Marie wondered if this was true. She decided to study the bottom of the ocean and see for herself.

When Marie was growing up, most girls did not attend college. They definitely didn't become scientists. Marie was not an average girl. She wanted to follow her heart. She wanted to do something she loved.

When she had the chance to attend college, she took it. She studied all the things she loved: rocks, maps, and oceans. She also met another scientist who wanted to study the ocean floor. Bruce and Marie made a great team.

Bruce and Marie decided to study what the ocean floor

looked like. They couldn't exactly go down to the bottom and check. The ocean is deep and very dark! Bruce went out in a boat and collected measurements on how deep the

ocean floor is. Why didn't Marie go on the boat? Back then, it was considered bad luck to have a woman on a research boat. Poor Marie! She was so smart, but had to do all the research from land.

Bruce sent his measurements back home to Marie. Marie was an expert mapmaker. Using just a pen and ruler, she drew out maps of the ocean floor.

Bruce and Marie's findings surprised everyone! The ocean floor was filled with canyons and mountain ranges, just like on land. Their findings supported the thoughts of an earlier scientist, Alfred Wegener.

He said that the continents and land were moving very slowly over time. Everyone thought he was crazy! But Marie could see it happening as she recorded the ocean data. Tiny ocean earthquakes were changing the shape of the land.

Most of the scientists didn't believe Marie. Famous ocean scientist Jacques Cousteau wanted to prove her wrong. He sent his fancy underwater cameras into the ocean to record data. What did he find? Marie was right! Finally, scientists started to believe this girl with big ideas.

Marie is still known as one of the best mapmakers in the world. Her work changed the way scientists thought about both land and oceans. She was smart and brave. Even though it wasn't easy, she worked hard to study the things that interested her. She made a BIG impact on how people think about oceans and land.

Lucky Peanuts

Building spaceships is really hard work. Building a spaceship that can land on the moon sounds even harder. That is what the people working at NASA in the 1960s were doing. They wanted to put the first astronaut on the moon. Before they could do that, they had to get a spaceship to launch and land on the moon. They were having a really hard time with this.

This was called the Ranger Project. They needed to have one of the Ranger spaceships land on the moon and take pictures. Then they could build a spaceship that would be safe to take a man to the moon. All of the Rangers kept crashing. The team had launched 6 Rangers that hadn't yet made it to the moon. They were having trouble with their mission. They were getting discouraged.

It was time to launch Ranger 7. The crew hoped this mission would be a success. They were

nervous. The crew's leader passed out a bag of peanuts to each member of the launch crew. He thought a snack might help ease the stress. It might make everyone feel a little better.

The rest is history! Ranger 7 was a successful mission. It launched, landed on the moon, and took the needed pictures. The team had a new and delicious tradition: lucky peanuts!

Since that day, peanuts have been at every NASA spaceship launch. They are even part of the unofficial checklist!

Usually the peanuts are in bags or jars. Once, the peanuts were red and green peanut M&M's to celebrate a Christmas Eve launch. Lucky peanuts are a fun tradition. They unite many years of people working together to explore space. Everyone loves a yummy snack!

What if you got to have a snack every time you tried something new and had to be brave? What would you choose?

Cockroaches Eat Moon Rocks?

Have you ever thought about how cool it would be to walk around on the moon? Neil Armstrong and Buzz Aldrin were the first astronauts to get to walk on the moon. It was exciting, but it was also probably a little scary.

The moon was still a mystery to scientists. They wanted to learn more about it. The best way to do this was to send people to the moon! They could gather information. They would help scientists learn more.

Scientists thought the moon was safe, but didn't know for sure. The astronauts had to be brave. When they landed on the moon, they had important work to do. They set up devices to help scientists study. They took a lot of photographs. They gathered up samples of moon rocks. These would be very important to scientists. They would learn if the moon was safe by studying these rocks.

Neil and Buzz brought back fifty pounds of moon rock to the scientists at NASA. What did they do with all that rock? They set up experiments. It was very important to be sure that the moon rocks wouldn't hurt people living on earth. Scientists wanted to keep studying the moon. They wanted to send other astronauts and learn more, but not if it was going to hurt people, plants, or animals on earth.

The NASA scientists set up a study. They gathered small groups to represent the creatures on earth. The two astronauts were also part of the study. They had to be quarantined as soon as they returned to earth. This meant they didn't get to go home to

their families right away. They stayed at the NASA base for three weeks. Scientists needed to be sure their moon trip hadn't made them sick.

Other animals, fish, birds, and plants were in the study, too. They were fed small bits of crushed-up moon rocks in their food. The plants had moon rocks crushed into their soil. The fish had moon rocks dropped into the water where they lived. Even a few cockroaches had moon dust sprinkled on their food! Scientists wanted to be sure nothing on earth would be harmed from their space research.

For three weeks, scientists watched the creatures carefully. They wanted to be sure they didn't get sick or die. This would mean that the moon rock might be made of something poisonous. Neil and Buzz were very interested in the study. They wanted to be able to go home and see their families!

All the plants, birds, bugs, animals, and fish were just fine at the end of the experiment. Some of the plants even grew better in the moon rock soil! The astronauts were able to return to their families. They had done a brave mission and helped scientists learn so much about the moon.

10

The Wright Brothers

Have you ever flown in an airplane? It is fun to soar up in the clouds. The first airplane was invented by two brothers, Wilbur and Orville Wright. When they were young, the brothers had a toy that would launch and fly. This gave them the idea for an airplane. They knew that when they got older they wanted to soar through the skies like that little toy.

When they got older, the brothers liked to work together on projects. They decided to move to North Carolina. The beaches made the perfect place to launch an airplane. They had wind, open space, and a soft, sandy place to land. They tinkered with the design of their airplane, the Wright Flyer. Finally, they thought it was ready to launch.

Which brother got to go up in the airplane for the launch? Good question! The brothers tossed a coin to see who would

fly first. Wilbur won the coin toss. The first day was not a success. They couldn't get the plane to fly. The Wright brothers didn't give up. They figured out what the problem was. They took the plane back to their shop and fixed the problem. When it was ready, they would try again.

The first airplane was made with wooden propellers. It had a small gas engine and fabric wings. There was a little place for the "pilot" to lay down and control where the plane would go. The first airplane did not look like the airplanes that you ride in today!

Three days after their first try, the brothers were ready again. This time it would be Orville who would fly the plane. Wilbur ran alongside as the airplane lifted off the ground. It flew for 120 feet! The brothers were so excited. Their plan had worked. This was just the beginning.

They spent all day flying the plane on the beach. Sadly, that is the only day the Wright Flyer was flown. At the end of the day, a strong gust of wind flipped the plane over. It broke the plane so it couldn't be used anymore. It didn't matter though. The Wright brothers now knew what was needed to fly!

The brothers made many more aircraft and flew many more times. Thanks to the Wright brothers, people can fly all over the world. They can even fly to the moon! Sixty-five years after the Wright brothers flew their airplane Neil Armstrong and Buzz Aldrin flew a spaceship to the moon. Neil took a small piece of fabric from the Wright Flyer in his pocket. He knew it would bring good luck!

The Wright brothers were creative. They used their brains in a special way. They were clever. Mostly they didn't give up. They tried hard, even when flying seemed impossible. It is important to try even when things are hard. You are a clever kid, too. What special things can you do?

11

Sweet Space Dreams

It would be awesome to be an astronaut. You might get to go to the moon. You'd see all those stars. You'd get to see Earth from your spaceship. Astronauts receive a bunch of training. They need to be able to work under pressure. They need to be able to handle being in really small spaces.

One astronaut, Scott Kelly, said he was tested to see if he could handle being in a small space. The researchers zipped him up in a small bag and put the bag in a closet. Then the people left him! He had no idea when they would come back. Scott wore a heart monitor. The researchers were checking his heart rate. If he was really nervous, his heart rate would go up. Luckily, Scott was able to stay calm under pressure. He was picked for the astronaut training program.

So why do astronauts need to be able to be in small spaces? There is not a lot of room on a spaceship. Astronauts need to be able to work, play, and sleep in a tiny space.

How do astronauts sleep in space? If they are in a space station, each astronaut is assigned their own "room." These rooms are actually really tiny, about the size of an old phone booth. At least the astronaut on a space station has his or her own space. Astronauts on a spaceship all have to share a sleeping space. It's like a sleepover every night!

There is no gravity in space, so astronauts have to be tied into their sleeping bags. Their sleeping bags are either tied or velcroed to the walls to keep them from floating away. Most astronauts have to sleep with earplugs and eye masks. The spacecraft can be really noisy. They are orbiting so fast that they can see fifteen sunrises in one night's sleep. That sounds

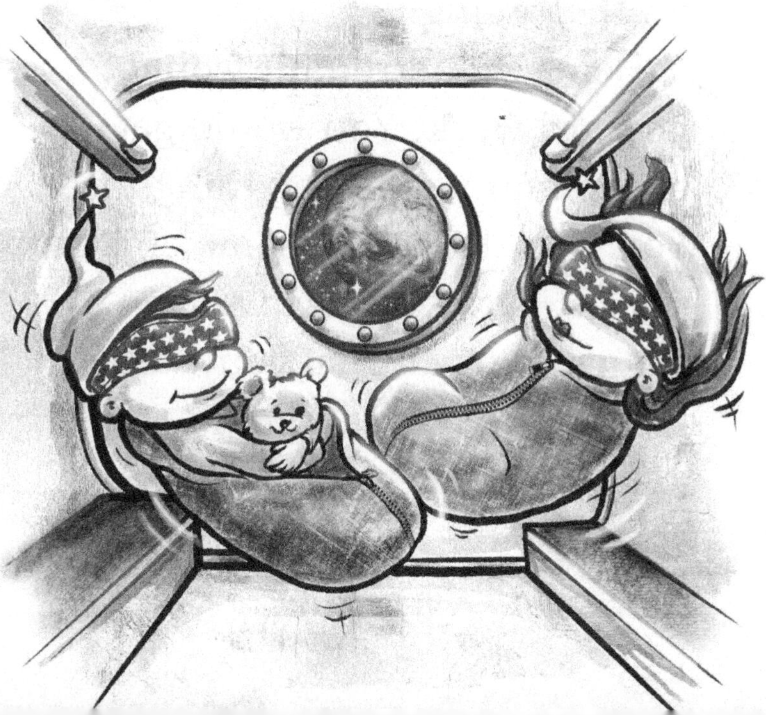

like it might be hard to get a good night's sleep!

Astronaut Nicole Stott said she actually slept best in space. She would let her sleeping bag float up the ceiling and sleep on the ceiling! She spent over one hundred nights in space and said it was the best sleep. Do you think you would sleep well on the ceiling?

Being an astronaut would be hard work. You would get to see many amazing things. You would sleep in some crazy places. Now you have a few things to practice if you want to head out in a spaceship!

12

Nice Shades!

If you lived near the North Pole thousands of years ago, what would be one of the most important inventions? Of course, fire and weapons to hunt were important. What about sunglasses?

Sunglasses seem like mostly a fashion accessory today. Thousands of years ago they were very important. If you lived in the Arctic, you were used to lots of snow. When the sun would shine, the snow would reflect it. That would make the snow seem really bright. It would become hard to see.

Sometimes the people that lived in the Arctic thousands

of years ago would have a problem. They would spend the day out hunting in the snow. After a few hours, they would suddenly go blind. They couldn't see anything! This was a real problem. It could take days for their eyesight to return to normal. What was causing this?

The condition is called snow blindness. Basically, the eye gets a sunburn. While the eye is healing from the sunburn, the person is blind. It usually lasts a few days. This would be a real pain today, but back then it was very dangerous. People couldn't see predators that might be hunting them. They couldn't find food or water. The snow was everywhere and could be on the ground for many months. What could they do?

Somebody came up with the idea for sunglasses. No, not the trendy glasses you would wear today! The first sunglasses looked a little different. They were carved out of wood or ivory. Small slits were carved to be the eyeholes. They had laces to tie around the head. These new glasses would keep the person wearing them from having to squint. They would be able to go out in the sun and snow without worrying about snow blindness.

Hunters would wear them when they would go out hunting. People would wear them on days when the sun seemed really bright. The invention of sunglasses really helped people thousands of years ago. They still help people today. It is good to protect your eyes from the sun's rays. Now we just get to look cool doing it!

What's that Chicken Doing on the Bridge?

John Roebling loved to build bridges. He had built many bridges all over the United States. Then John had a new idea. He came up with a clever plan. He wanted to build the longest bridge in the world.

Nobody else thought it could be done.

Luckily, John's son, Washington Roebling, liked the idea, too. They worked together on the project. They wanted to build a bridge connecting Manhattan and Brooklyn in New York. It would have to cross the East River. The river was very wide. No one thought a bridge could be that long.

John and Washington found a few people who believed in them. They decided to see if they could do it. They got to work on the bridge.

One day, John hurt his foot while working. His foot

got infected and made John very sick. He ended up dying. It was sad, but Washington still wanted to complete the project. He kept working. For years, Washington and his crew worked on the bridge. Some of the crew had to work underwater while they were building the bridge. The air pressure used

underwater could make the workers sick. Washington was one of the workers who got really sick. It became hard for him to walk. He couldn't go to the bridge to help the workers anymore.

Washington really wanted to complete the bridge. His wife, Emily, wanted to help. Emily was very smart, just like her husband. They worked together on the plans. Washington could view the bridge through his telescope from his bedroom window. He and Emily would figure out what needed to happen. Then Emily would go to the work site and tell the workers what to do. Emily was a very important part of the bridge being finished. She had to solve many problems while the bridge was being built. She became the leader of the whole project.

The Brooklyn Bridge was finally finished in 1883, after thirteen years of building. The clever plan had worked. The Brooklyn Bridge was the longest bridge in the world. There was a big party for the new bridge. People gave speeches, sang songs, and shot fireworks. Emily was the first person to ride across the bridge. She rode in her carriage and carried a rooster on her lap. The rooster was a sign of victory.

Even though they faced many challenges, the builders of the Brooklyn Bridge never gave up. People told them it was not possible. They tried anyway. Washington and Emily believed in the project so much that they kept going even after Washington got sick. Never give up if it is something you really believe in!

No Snow? No problem!

Do you like to play in the snow? Do you ever wish you could make it snow whenever you felt like it? Many years ago, some people figured out how to make snow.

In America in the early 1900s, snow skiing was a popular sport. Many people would spend their vacations going snow skiing. They would go to snow skiing resorts. They would stay in cabins and ski down the snowy hills. It was a lot of fun. The owners of the resorts made a lot of money. People loved to be able to snow ski.

What would happen if it didn't snow? People would be disappointed to have their plans ruined. Nature can be unpredictable. Sometimes in the winter it can be very cold and still doesn't snow!

In 1934, the Toronto Ski Club had a big ski jumping competition planned. But guess what? No snow! The people running the event had to get creative. They decided to try something new. They took all the ice from the local ice skating rink. They turned that ice into shaved ice and put it down on the big ski hill. It worked! The

skiers got some of their best jumps ever.

Several years later it was New Year's Eve. A big ski resort was packed with guests. It was cold, but there was no snow on the ski slopes. The resort owner was starting to get nervous. He wanted people to be able to ski. He decided to see if he could make his own snow. He bought 450 tons of ice. He rented a wood chipper. He put all that ice through the wood chipper and made his own snow for the slopes! The skiers got to enjoy the slopes. The resort made money with happy skiers.

Three friends were all skiers and engineers. They thought snow could be made easier than making tons of shaved ice. They thought about the two things that it takes to make snow in nature. It takes cold air and water. Winter usually has lots of cold air.

The friends got to work. They invented a machine that used air pressure and water pressure. A droplet of water got blasted into the cold air. The droplet broke into smaller pieces and froze. This created snow! At last, people could create snow using just cold air and water!

Today, most ski resorts use this technique to make snow when nature doesn't. The extra snow can make the ski seasons longer. It can be used when ski hills get too icy. Skiers everywhere like these snow machines. Now, if only you could get one in your backyard!

15

Human Computers?

Are you good at math? I'll bet you are pretty smart! Are you as smart as a computer?

Back in the 1950s, there were three women who were so smart that they were sometimes called human computers! They were math whizzes. They used just a pencil and paper to solve really hard math problems.

These three women all worked together for the space program at NASA. During the 1950s, Black people and White people weren't allowed to work together. These three women were Black. They worked together in the West Area Computers with other Black women. They were very smart, but it wasn't always easy for them. Some people judged them by the color of their skin. They had to work harder to prove that they were smart and capable.

Dorothy Vaughn was a leader. When NASA started using computers, she knew that it was important work. She knew

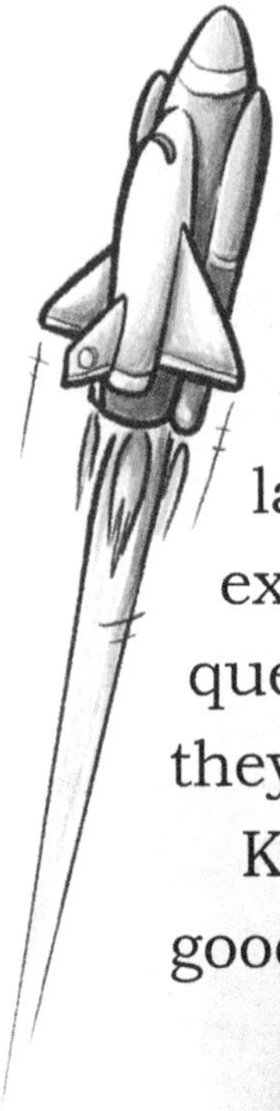

that computers would help her in her job. She learned computer programming, which is basically how to speak the computer language. She became an expert. When NASA had questions about computers, they would always ask Dorothy.

Katherine Johnson was really good at solving math equations.

She had to solve math equations to help put the first American astronaut in space. She was on the team that helped put astronauts on the moon for the first time. John Glenn was a famous astronaut. He felt better when Katherine checked the work needed to launch his spaceship. He trusted her more than he trusted the computers.

Mary Jackson loved math and science. She wanted to be an engineer. An engineer is a scientist. They help make planes and spaceships fly. This was when Black students couldn't go to school with White students. Mary had to get special permission to go to engineering school. She worked really hard. Mary became the first Black female engineer at NASA. She liked to help other women that were smart in science and math. She helped other women become engineers for NASA.

These talented women had brains that were smart like computers. They didn't let any challenges slow them down. They worked hard to show the world all the things they could do. When you face challenges it's important to remember that you are smart. You are clever and capable. You have many talents. You can do anything you put your mind to, even if it is a little hard sometimes.

My Snack Melted!

What is your favorite snack to eat? Do you like to eat fruit? Maybe you like to pop some popcorn in the microwave and munch on that. Did you know that the microwave was invented thanks to a melted snack?

Percy Spencer was a really smart guy. He liked to work on problems. He liked to find simple answers for problems that seemed really hard. Percy worked for a company that made tools for the military. One day, Percy was at work. He was trying to make one of the radar tools better. He wanted to make it more powerful. He was using tiny electromagnetic waves. These waves are sometimes known as microwaves.

Percy was worn out from all the hard work. He decided it was time for a snack break. He reached into his pocket. Percy always carried a yummy peanut cluster with him in his pocket. It was a tasty snack. Percy loved nature and sometimes he would share his peanut cluster with the squirrels.

When Percy opened his snack, he found that it had melted. Percy said, "It was a sticky, gooey mess!"

This had never happened before. Percy thought it must be

because of the tiny microwaves he was working with that day.

Percy was curious. He wanted to know more. He placed an egg under the tube he was working on. The egg exploded! Percy got some popcorn kernels. The tube popped the kernels and Percy shared popcorn with everyone in the office. The idea for the microwave had been born.

Can you believe it took almost twenty years before the microwave became popular? The first microwaves were too big and cost too much money. It took some time before microwaves were made small and cheap. Now almost every home has one in their kitchen. Microwaves sure make heating up our favorite snacks quick and easy!

The Clumsy Cook

Have you ever felt clumsy? Josephine Dickson was always feeling clumsy in the kitchen. She really liked to cook, but sometimes she would cut herself with a knife or burn herself on a pan. It was never anything bad, but it was annoying. She wanted to cover up the wound, but no companies made small bandages. Wrapping the big bandages was a pain! They were just too big.

Josephine shared her problem with her husband, Earle. He worked for the company Johnson & Johnson. They made a lot of first aid supplies, like gauze and tape. He thought maybe he could make something to help his

wife. He unrolled some long surgical tape. Then he stuck a little gauze in the middle of the tape. Josephine helped him re-roll this new bandage. She could unroll a tiny piece and stick it on anytime she cut herself. They had just invented the first band-aid!

Have you ever used a band-aid? They are pretty helpful to have when we get hurt. If you scrape your knee or cut your finger, a band-aid is very useful. Josephine and Earle sure thought so. They told Earle's boss about their invention. He liked the idea. Johnson & Johnson started to make band-aids to sell. At first, nobody bought the new invention. People weren't sure what to make of it. Sometimes people don't like new ideas. It takes them a while to get used to something new.

One year, the Boy Scouts put band-aids in all of their first aid kits. Finally, people saw how useful they were! Now every home has a package of band-aids just in case someone gets hurt. It all started with a husband and wife who had a tiny problem and wanted to solve it. Even tiny things can help in a big way!

YOUR REVIEW

What if I told you that just one minute out of your life could bring joy and jubilation to everyone working at a kids book company?

What am I yapping about? I'm talking about leaving this book a review.

I promise you, we take them **VERY seriously**. Don't believe me?

Each time right after someone just like you leaves this book a review, a little siren goes off right here in our office. And when it does we all pump our fists with pure happiness.

A disco ball pops out of the ceiling, flashing lights come on... it's party time!

Roger, our marketing guy, always and I mean always, starts flossing like a crazy person and keeps it up for awhile. He's pretty good at it. (It's a silly dance he does, not cleaning his teeth)

Sarah, our office manager, runs outside and gives everyone up and down the street high fives. She's always out of breath when she comes back but it's worth it!

Our editors work up in the loft and when they hear the review siren, they all jump into the swirly slide and ride down into a giant pit of marshmallows where they roll around and make marshmallow angels. (It's a little weird, but tons of fun)

So reviews are a pretty big deal for us.

It means a lot and helps others just like you who also might enjoy this book, find it too.

You're the best!

From all of us goofballs at Big Dreams Kids Books

Made in United States
Orlando, FL
27 May 2024

47266429R10055